Introduction to Basic Accounting

CA Tarannum Khatri

ISBN:
9781983015403

INTRODUCTION

Hi,

Thanks for purchasing this book!

I am Tarannum Khatri. I am Chartered Accountant and working in finance field for more than 10 years. I am also finance instructor on udemy and other online learning platforms.

My motive to write this book is to provide simple explanation about accounting basic. After reading this book, please share your view about this book on review section on Amazon. Your suggestions for improvement are also welcomed.

Thanks,

Tarannum

TABLE OF CONTENTS

What is accounging?   1

Benefits of accounting   2

Accounting Principles   3

Accouting Principles applied in financial statements   8

Accounting terms   10

ACCOUNTING EQUATION   14

Accounting cycle   22

Debit and credits, Journal entry and T account   25

Posting into ledger – T account and balancing ledger   32

Preparation of unadjusted trial balance   37

Adjusting entries   39

Adjusted trial balance   50

Preparation of 10 column worksheet   55

Preparation of financial statements   58

Cash Flow statement   67

Post closing trial balance   76

Speciall Offer   77

WHAT IS ACCOUNTING?

Accounting is process of recording financial transactions in presentable manner. Many activities are linked together in accounting like storing, sorting, retrieving, summarizing and presenting.

Financial accounting: Financial accounting relates to presenting information to outside of the company via financial reports. These reports are prepared as per acceptable accounting principles – GAAP or US GAAP.

Management accounting: Accounting helps management to provide necessary data and reports which helps them to take important decisions in business. Reports which referred to budgets, estimates, and internal analytics are covered in management accounting. These reports are not distributed to outside of the company.

Accounting as per regulations:

Income tax regulations also require maintaining accounts and submitting the reports.

BENEFITS OF ACCOUNTING

Verifiable Data:
Big advantage of accounting is verifiable data. It is not biased or based on someone's opinion. But accounting is based on generally accounting principles. The beauty of accounting is its comparability. You can compare result of company with previous year or with result of competitive company.

Reliable:
You can rely on accounting result. You can verify each asset, liability, debts or result of business.

Example. You see $1000 debt in your balance sheet. You can verify it through ledger balances and bank statement. You can also find reason of debt and purpose of debt through various bills and vouchers. That's why accounting is reliable system and followed by whole world.

Provides analytical data:
Accounting provides analytical reports referred as profit and loss account or income statement, balance sheet, cash flow statements. This analysis is helpful to management, lenders, shareholders, owners, employees of business.

ACCOUNTING PRINCIPLES

There are some rules to write accounts and we call them accounting principles. Accounting principles give financial statements comparability and reliability. In many cases, it is required that Accounting is based on acceptable accounting principles based on GAAP and independent audit report is necessary for it.

Following are the main accounting principles used in day to day accounting:

1. **Entity assumption:**
   Entity assumption is applicable for proprietorship business. As per entity assumption, business and business owner are different entities and transactions of business and transactions of owners are considered separately.

   Due to this assumption, we show capital of proprietor on liability side of balance sheet. Separate entries are made when owner withdraws money from business for personal purposes or when he introduces money in business.

2. **Time period assumption:**
   Result of business is measured for specific time period. Annual and quarterly reports are prepared and published when required. This assumption gives comparability to financial statements.

3. **Going concern principle:**
   It is assumption that company will continue its business long run and there is no intention of company to

3

liquidate. Certain expenses are deferred and prepared expenses are not considered in current year in line with going concern assumption.

If company has intention to close the business in short run, it is required to mention that fact in notes in financial statements.

4. Materiality Principle:

Materiality principle allows accountant to violate other accounting principles if it is not material for company. Material means having monetary value or importance of company. It is judgmental decision of accountant to test transaction with regards to materiality.

Example:
$1000 is expensed to purchase fixed asset.

For small business, $1000 is material and it should be capitalized. For multi-million dollar company, it is not material item and can be expensed.

Important matter is that the result of business should not be misleading due to decision.

Rounding off to nearest dollar is also example of materiality principle.

5. Monetary Unit assumption:

This principle allows recording and preparing accounts in specific currency. Inflation or deflation of currency is totally ignored while comparing result of past years with current years.

6. Matching principle:

The expenses should be matched with revenue as per

this principle. This is based on accrual accounting. We record income and expenses when they are accrued and not when cash is paid or received.

Example:

Company has sales of $10000 for month of January. To get that sale, company has outstanding $1000 commission. Company paid $800 in January and $200 in February. As per matching principle, Company will match $1000 expense with $10000 revenue and Show profit of January as $9000. It is immaterial that $200 is outstanding to pay in January.

7. Revenue recognition principle:

This principle requires company to record sales when it is accrued – goods are disposed. It is immaterial whether money is received or not. Recording of transaction is done when it is due and not when money is exchanged.

Example:
TYK Ltd made $10,000 sale for December. Out of which $2000 is receivable and $8000 is received.

Based on revenue recognition principle, TYK Ltd should recognize $10000 sale in December month.

Revenue recognition principle helps to show true result of business. You can see difference in profits in two different accounting method – cash accounting and accrual accounting from below example.

Example:

Result as per Accrual accounting

Expense	$	$	Income	$	$
Administration Exp			Sales		
Paid	9,000				
Payable	1,000	10,000	Received	50,000	
Commission			Receivable	10,000	60,000
Paid	500				
Payable	100	600			
Profit		**49,400**			
		60,000			60,000

Results as per Cash accounting

Expense	$	$	Income	$	$
Administration Exp			Sales		
Paid	9,000				
Payable	1,000	9,000	Received	50,000	
Commission			Receivable	10,000	50,000
Paid	500				
Payable	100	500			
Profit		**41,500**			
		50,000			50,000

8. Cost principle:

Cost principle required company to show its asset at purchase price. Any price increase in market price of asset is ignored. Inflation is not considered.

Example:

Company purchased Land at $100000 on 1st March, 2013. On 31st March, 2014, the land price increased and market price of land reached to $110000. Company should ignore this increase and show value of land as $100000.

9. Full disclosure principle:

It is necessary to disclose all significant information in financial statements which affects decision of stakeholders. There is foot note section to provide all necessary information not covered in financial statements.

Example:

Change in accounting method, change in method of valuation of stock, Law suit pending against the company are required to shown in line with full disclosure principle.

10. Conservatism

Conservatism principle requires company to consider all the possible losses in business but ignore all the possible gains. Due to this principle, accountant shows possible losses under footnote in financial statements but does not show possible financial gains.

ACCOUNTING PRINCIPLES APPLIED IN FINANCIAL STATEMENTS:

Balance sheet as on 31st March, 2016

Liability	$	Asset	$
Capital of Mr. John	8,00,000	Land	6,50,000
Secured loan	1,00,000	Cash	1,200
Unsecured loan	20,000	Bank	40,000
Creditors	12,000	Stock	22,000
		Debtor	1,68,800
		Furniture	50,000
	9,32,000		9,32,000

Profit and loss account for the year ending 31st March, 2016

Loss	$	Income	$
Purchase	70,000	Sales	1,00,000
Interest on loan	1,000		
Rent	4,000		
Depreciation on furniture	5,000		
Profit transferred	25,000		
	1,00,000		1,00,000
Loss	$	Income	$

Note:

Law suit worth $1000 is pending against company.

Now, we check each Accounting assumption from above table:

1. Entity assumption: Capital of john is shown on liability side.
2. Time period principle: Profit and loss account is prepared for 1 year period.
3. Monetary unit assumption: Figures are shown in $.
4. Conservatism assumption: Law suit is shown in footnote.
5. Matching principle: Expenses of the year are matched with revenue earned during the year.
6. Revenue recognition: All revenue received or receivable is shown in profit and loss account.
7. Cost principle: Land is shown on cost.
8. Going concern: Depreciation is charged on furniture expecting continuance of business.
9. Full disclosure and materiality: Law suit is shown in footnote.

ACCOUNTING TERMS

Before you start reading and studying books, check out following accounting terms used in business. It will be easy for you to understand next chapters once you understand them.

Accounting
Accounting is keeping records of transaction for analysis purpose and to provide reports to internal and external parties.

AuditOr
Auditor verifies accuracy and completeness of financial records with supporting documents and papers. Audit which is performed by outside person is external audit and audit performed by person from the organization is internal audit.

Profit and loss account
It is financial statement showing expense and income of the business for particular period.

Balance sheet
It is financial statement showing assets, liability and capital of business on a specific date. (year end or quarterly)

Cash flow statement
It is financial statements showing movement of cash in business. Cash has broad meaning in cash flow statement which covers bank also.

Revenue
It is the income of the business from sale of service or

goods.

Accounting equation
Asset − Liability = capital. Accounting equation balances with accurate accounting.

Account payable
Money owed to others or creditors.

Accounts receivable
Money owed to business by others or Debtors.

Accrual accounting
Recording financial transactions when transaction occurs and not when money is exchanged.

Cash basis accounting
In cash basis accounting, financial transactions are recorded when cash is received or disbursed.

Credit
Right column of the accounts.

Debit
Left column of accounts.

Depreciation
Writing of assets' value during life of the asset.

Dividend
Profit given to shareholders of company.

Goodwill
Intangible asset of company due to its brand popularity.

Invoice
It is received or issued while purchasing or selling.

Liquid assets
They are assets that can be easily converted to cash.

Loans
Money borrowed or lent.

Non operating income
Income not generated from business activity.

Operating income
Income generated from business activity.

Payroll
It is account showing employees and their wages / salaries in account.

Reconciliation
The act of verifying two sets of records to ensure accuracy of figures.

Example:

Process of Verification of creditor's payment with bank ledger is reconciliation.

Process of Verification of bank ledger with passbook is reconcillation.

Objective of reconciliation is prevention of fraud.

Retained earning

Statement of account
Document issued by supplier to its customer is statement of accounts. It will include details of invoice, payment details and discount details.

Single entry bookkeeping
It means recording any transaction by one entry. Generally small business owners use it having few cash transactions.

Double entry book keeping
It means recording any transaction by two entry- debit and credit.

Asset
It means property of business. Example: cash, bank, fixed asset, stock, receivable. They are items owned by business and would give benefit to business in future.

Liability
It is obligations of entity to owner of business and person outside.

Budgeting
It is estimation of costs, revenues and resources for specified period. It helps in planning, setting standard and controlling expense.

Book keeping
Recording financial transaction is bookkeeping.

Capital
Capital is amount invested by owner of the business in business. For proprietorship, it is amount invested by proprietor. For corporate, it is amount invested by shareholders.

ACCOUNTING EQUATION

Accounting equation is base on which accounting system is constructed. Accounting equation simplifies relation among capital, asset and liability. Accounting equation is

$$Assets = Liabilities + Capital\ (Equity)$$

In each transaction of business, above equation is always balanced.

Accounting Equation Rules for sample transaction:

Purchase Fixed asset	Fixed asset increases	Bank decreases
Sell Fixed asset	Fixed asset decreases	Bank increases
Money received from debtor	Debtor decreases	Bank increases
Pay supplier	Supplier decreases	Bank decreases
Pay salary	Bank decreases	Capital decreases
Sell goods on credit	Capital increases	Debtor increases
Sell service on cash	Capital increases	Bank increases
Drawing by owner	Capital decreases	Bank decreases
Capital introduced by owner	Capital increases	Bank increases

Example with sample transactions and accounting equations:

2015	
1st April	Mr. Smart starts business with $120000.
2nd April	Purchases laptop $1,000.
15th April	Provide service $2500 on credit.
3rd June	Receives due of service - $2500.
31st July	Purchases new software $ 20000.
1st August	Provide online service and receives payment $5000
31st August	Paid virtual assistant $200 for service
22nd February	Withdraw $1000 from business for personal use
31st March	Provides online consultancy $20000

Accounting equations of above transactions and effect on balance sheet:

1st april, 2015 : started business with capital of $12,00,000.

Asset	=liability +	capital	
$1200000	= 0 +	12,00,000	Capital increases and bank balance increases

Position in balance sheet

Asset	$	Liabilities	$
Bank	12,00,000	Capital	12,00,000

2nd April, 2015 : Purchases laptop at $1000.

Asset	=liability +	capital	
$1000 - $1000	= 0 +	0	Fixed asset increases and bank balance Decreases

Effect in balance sheet

Asset	$	Liabilities	$
Bank	11,99,000	Capital	12,00,000
Fixed asset	1000		
Total effect	0		0

15th april, 2015 Provide online service $2500 on credit.

In this case, though money is not received, it is required to show transaction in books of accounts as per accrual accounting principle.

Asset	=liability +	capital	
Debtor		Revenue	
$2500	= 0 +	$2500	Debtor increases and profit transferred to capital

Effect in balance sheet

Asset	$	Liabilities	$
Debtor	2500	Capital 12,00,000 +2,500	12,02,500
Bank	11,99,000		
Fixed asset	1,000		
Total effect	12,02,500		12,02,500

3rd June, 2015: Receives due of service- $2500.

On receiving money for outstanding, debtor balance reduces and bank balance increases.

Asset	Asset	=liability +	capital
Debtor	Bank		Revenue
-$2500	$2500	= 0 +	0

Effect in balance sheet

Asset	$	Liabilities	$
Debtor 2500- 2500	0	Capital 12,00,000 +2,500	12,02,500
Bank 11,99,000+2500	12,01,500		
Fixed asset	1,000		
Total effect	12,02,500		12,02,500

You can understand from above transactions that there are two possibilities in accounting equation.

1. There is a change in both sides of equation.

2. Transaction effect is nullified due to conversion of one asset (Debtor) into another asset (cash) or one liability into another liability.

31st July, 2015 Purchases new software at $20000.

In this transaction, fixed asset (New software) increases and bank balance decreases.

Asset	Asset	Asset	=liability +	Capital
Debtor	Bank	Software		Revenue
	-$20,000	$20,000	= 0 +	0

Effect on balance sheet:

Asset	$	Liabilities	$
Debtor 2500- 2500	0	Capital 12,00,000 +2,500	12,02,500
Bank 11,99,000+2500- 20000	11,81,500		
Fixed asset 1000+20000	21,000		
Total effect	12,02,500		12,02,500

1st august, 2015 Fees receives for online service - $5000

Asset	Asset	=liability +	capital
Debtor	Bank	=	Revenue
	$5000	= 0 +	$5000

Effect in balance sheet

Asset	$	Liabilities	$
Debtor 2500- 2500	0	Capital 12,00,000 +2,500+5,000	12,07,500
Bank 11,99,000+2500- 20000 + 5,000	11,86,500		

Fixed asset 1000+20000	21,000		
Total effect	12,07,500		12,07,500

31st August, 2015 pays $200 to virtual assistant for service.

Since money is paid to virtual assistant, assets decrease. The second effect is $200 decrease in owner's equity.

Asset	Asset	=liability +	capital
Debtor	Bank	=	Expense
	-$200	= 0 +	-$200

Effect in balance sheet

Asset	$	Liabilities	$
Debtor 2500- 2500	0	Capital 12,00,000 +2,500+5,000-200	12,07,300
Bank 11,99,000+2500- 20000 + 5,000-200	11,86,300		
Fixed asset 1000+20000	21,000		
Total effect	12,07,300		12,07,300

Exercise:

Make accounting equation of last two transactions given below:

| 22nd February | Withdraw $1000 from business for personal use |
| 31st March | Provides online consultancy $20000 |

ACCOUNTING CYCLE

Accounting is system and step by step process to classify, record and summarize financial transactions. This process is called accounting cycle. Some steps are not followed in computerized environment but understanding whole accounting cycle help you to do accurate accounting.

Accounting cycle may be monthly, quarterly, annually but the process involved remains same.

ACCOUNTING CYCLE

Steps in accounting cycle:

1. Transaction and journalize transaction: Accounting cycle starts with transaction. Transaction should be financial. Sale, purchase, money received from debtor, sale return etc. is financial transaction. All these transactions are recorded in journal ledger. Journal is called books of original entry. In computerized accounting software, transaction is direct posted in ledger from making invoice or voucher in software and this step is skipped.

2. Posting transaction in ledger- T account: Second step is posting transaction from journal to ledger or T account. T account is summary of all the transactions related to single account for certain period. In computerized account, this step is automatic and done by computer.

3. Preparation of unadjusted trial balance: The trial balance is a list of all accounts of company. The total debit balance equals total credit balance. Unadjusted trial balance means trial balance that is prepared before doing adjustment entries in accounts.

4. Preparation of worksheet: In large companies, there are lots of adjustments. In this situation, accountant prepare 10 column worksheet to do adjustment and prepare adjusted trial balance.

5. Preparation of adjusting entries: After preparing trial balance, all the remaining adjustments are recorded through adjusting entries. Depreciation, payable,

receivable, any errors are recorded via adjusting entries.

6. Preparation of adjusted trial balance: Once all the adjusting entries are recorded, accountant prepares adjusted trial balance. Balances of adjusted trial balance reflect in financial statements.

7. Preparation of financial statements: Financial statements include profit and loss account and balance sheet, Cash Flow statement. Financial statements are reports about company's financial results, financial conditions and cash movements.

8. Do closing entries: All the incomes and revenue accounts are closed at year end via closing entries.

9. Post closing trial balance: Post closing trial balance including effect of closing entries are prepared.

DEBIT AND CREDITS, JOURNAL ENTRY AND T-ACCOUNT

In double entry system, each transaction is recorded in two accounts and there are two entries related to any transaction.

Debit
Debit means writing on debit side of account.

Credit
Credit means writing on credit side of account.

Abbreviation of Debit is Dr and Abbreviation of Credit is Cr.

Remember following rules to correctly determine which account should be debited and which account should be credited for a transaction:

1. When asset increases, debit the asset account.

2. When asset decreases, credit the asset account.

3. When liability increases, credit the liability account.

4. When liability decreases, debit the liability account.

5. When there is income or profit or gain, credit the income account.

6. When there is loss or expense, debit the loss account.

Recognition of accounts involved in transaction is first step to do write entry in account. After that you can apply above rules for accurate accounting.

Asset account	
Debit the purchase	Credit the sale

Liability account	
Debit the purchase	Credit the sale

Income account	
	Credit when there is profit or gain

Expense account	
Debit when there is expense or loss	

Sample transaction and debit and credit effect

1. Company purchases new machinery at $10000 by cheque.

   Effect: as machinery balance increases, we debit the machinery account and other side bank balance reduces, so we credit bank account.

Machinery account (Asset account)

To bank account	$10,000		

Bank account

		By machinery account	$10,000

Journal entry:

Journal entry means writing transaction in *Journal*.

Generally in computerized accounting, transaction occurs in software for sale, purchase or expense and transfers directly to ledger account. However, adjustments after year end are done through journal entries.

For above transaction, we write entry in following manner in journal.

Date	Marchinery a/c Dr	10,000	
	To bank a/c		10,000

2. Company takes $120000 loan.

In this transaction, company's bank balance increases so we will debit bank account. Other side, loan account increases so we credit loan account.

Bank account

To loan account $1,20,000	

Loan account

	By bank account $1,20,000

Journal entry

Date	Bank a/c Dr	1,20,000	
	To loan a/c		1,20,000

3. Company sales goods on credit $30,000.

Explanation: in this transaction, income (sale) increases so we credit the sale account and debtors (asset) increases so we debit the debtor account.

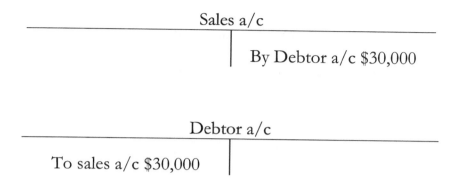

Sales a/c

By Debtor a/c $30,000

Debtor a/c

To sales a/c $30,000

Journal entry

Date	Debtor a/c Dr	30,000	
	To sales a/c		30,000

4. Proprietor withdraws fund from business for personal use- $2000.

    Exp. As per entity principle, it is required to record transaction of proprietor with business separately.

    In above transaction, bank decreases so we credit the bank account and on other side, drawing account increases so we debit drawing account. We transfer drawing account to capital account at the end of the year.

Bank account

By drawing account

	$2000

Drawing account

To bank $2000	

Journal entry

Date	Drawing a/c Dr	2,000	
	To bank a/c		2,000

5. Company pays the salary $20000.

Exp. In this transaction, there is expense so we debit salary account and other side, bank decreases so we credit the bank account.

Bank account

	By salary $20,000

Salary account

To bank $20,000	

Journal entry

Date	Salary a/c Dr	20,000	
	To bank a/c		20,000

Exercise:

Prepare T account for following transactions:

1. Interest received in bank - $56.

2. Electricity bill paid - $560.

3. Cash sale made - $2000.

4. Capital introduced in business - $50,000.

5. Debts paid off- $2200.

POSTING INTO LEDGER -T ACCOUNT
AND BALANCING LEDGER

Once all the transactions are recorded in T account, next step is to find balance of T account / ledger account.

Let's understand with following simple example:

Date	Transaction
June 2015	
1	Cash sale of $50000.
15	Credit sale of $2000.
30	Salary paid -$20000.
30	Loan receives from bank - $100000.

Ledger:

Bank account

2015		$	2015		$
1st June	To sale	50,000	30th june	By salary a/c	20,000
30th June	To loan	1,00,000	30th June	By balance c/d	1,30,000
		1,50,000			**1,50,000**
1st July	To balance c/d	1,30,000			

How to find balance of T-account?

Once all the transactions are posted in T-accounts. Following procedure needs to be done to balancing the ledger.

1. When account has only credit entries or debit entries, balancing is easy. Sum of the debit entries or credit entries is balance of the ledger.
2. When account has credit entries and debit entries, do sum of the both sides' entries and enter larger figure as total of ledger.
3. Calculate balance by deducting larger figure from

smaller figure. Write that figure on side which has smaller total. Write balance c/d (carried down) against it.

4. Brought down that figure on opposite side in next period.

In computerized software, balancing is done automatic by software. However, learning the process will clear your accounting concept.

In above example,$1,50,000 has come into bank account and $20,000 has gone so the balance of bank account is $1, 05,000-$20,000= $ 1, 30,000. This closing balance will become opening debit balance for succeeding period.

Sales account

2015		$	2015		$
30th june	To balance c/d	**7,000**	1th June	By cash a/c	5000
			15th June	By debtor a/c	2000
		7000			**7000**
			1st July	By balance b/d	7,000

Balance in sales account is $7,000. As there is no

transaction posted on debit side, we consider sum of credit side as balance for sales account.

Loan a/c

2015			2015		
30th June	To balance c/d	**1,00,000**	30th June	By bank a/c	1,00,000
		1,00,000			1,00,000
			1st July	By balance b/d	1,00,000

There is only one transaction in loan account. The amount $1,00,000 is credit balance of loan account.

Here is the summary of normal balances in T-account we find.

Account	Normal balances
Asset	Debit
Liability	Credit
Expense	Debit
Income	Credit

Capital or owner's equity	Capital
Drawing account	Debit
Losses	Debit
Gain	Credit

PREPARATION OF UNADJUSTED TRIAL BALANCE

Unadjusted trial balance is list presenting all the accounts and their pre adjustment balances. The balances are brought forward from ledger accounts.

Purpose of preparation of trial balance:

Preparing trial balance for company helps it to detect any mathematical errors or omissions that have occurred in double entry accounting system.

Format:

There are three columns in trial balance:

1. Name of account

2. Debit

3. Credit

On left column, debit balances of accounts are listed and on right column, credit balances of accounts are listed.

Generally following order of account is used in trial balance:

1. Assets and liabilities

2. Equity accounts

3. Income and expense accounts

Trial balance is showing position of accounts on reporting

dates.

How to prepare trial balance?

Preparation of trial balance is really easy. We need to post balance from each account to left side if there is debit balance and right side if there is credit balance.

Following is the sample trial balance:

Account	Dr	Cr
Land	1,20,000	
Furniture	10,000	
Stock	12,000	
Creditor		22,000
Debtor	52,000	
Loan given to Z	22,000	
Bills payable		10,000
Loan received		1,12,000
Owner's equity		72,000
	2,16,000	**2,16,000**

In trial balance, debits always equal credits if accounting is accurate.

ADJUSTING ENTRIES

Adjusting entries are journal entries recorded after preparation of unadjusted trial balance. Adjustments are made to follow accrual principles of accounting and comply with IFRS and GAAP.

There are generally three types of adjusting entries:

1. Accruals: To record the revenue or expenses which have not been recorded but which have been already occurs or due in accounting period.

2. Deferrals: To defer the revenue or expenses which have been recorded but which have not been occurs or due in accounting period.

3. Provisions or reserves: Reserves are created for doubtful debts, obsolescence inventory or for investment fluctuation.

Here is the list of general adjusting entries:

1. To record payable or receivables.

2. To write of depreciation

3. To record prepaid expense

4. To record any accrued income.

5. To record loss on sale of fixed asset

6. To write off obsolescence inventory

7. To write off bad debt

8. To create various provisions.

9. To record bank charges not recorded in account

Effect of adjustment entries:

Adjusting entries involve profit and loss account and balance sheet.

Adjusting entries example:

1. Z ltd has recorded $20000 depreciation on building having book value $2,00,000.

Depreciation a/c Dr	20000	
To Building		20000

In above example, adjustment entry for depreciation is recorded by debit depreciation and credit building. Depreciation is expense so we debit it. We will credit building to reduce its value. (Asset's value is reduced by crediting it.).

Let's see how this adjustment reflects in ledger, balance sheet and profit and loss account.

Depreciation a/c

Date	Particular	$	Date	Particular	$
31/3/15	To building	20,000	31/3/15	**By P & L a/c**	**20,000**
		20,000			20,000

Building

Date	Particular	$	Date	Particular	$
1/4/14	To balance b/d	2,00,000	31/3/15	By Depreciation a/c	20,000
			31/3/15	By balance c/d	**1,80,000**
		2,00,000			2,00,000

Profit and loss account

Expense	$	Income	$
Depreciation	20,000		

Balance sheet

Asset	$	Liability	$
Fixed Asset 20,00,000			
Less Dep. 20,000			
	19,80,000		

2. Z ltd. has $10000 revenue which has been unbilled.

Ans.

Debtor a/c Dr	10,000	
To Income a/c		10,000

In above transaction, we do adjusting entries by debiting debtor account and crediting income account.

Reflection in ledgers and financial statement:

Debtor a/c

Date	Particular	$	Date	Particular	$
1/4/14	To balance b/d	50,000	31/3/15	**By balance c/d**	**60,000**
31/3/15	To Income a/c	10,000			
		60,000			60,000

Income a/c

Date	Particular	$	Date	Particular	$
31/3/15	To P&L a/c	4,30,000	1/4/14	By bank a/c	4,20,000
			31/3/15	By debtor a/c	**10,000**
		2,00,000			4,30,000

Profit and loss account

Expense	$	Income	$
		Income a/c	10,000

Balance sheet

Asset	$	Liability	$
Debtor	10,000		

3. Z Ltd. has paid $15000 as insurance. Among which, $2000 is related to next financial year.

Entry.

Insurance paid in advance a/c Dr	$2,000	
To Insurance exp a/c		$2,000

We have done adjusting entry by debiting insurance paid in advance a/c and crediting insurance exp a/c. By debiting insurance paid in advance account, we have created asset and by crediting insurance expense account, we have reduced insurance expense by amount not related to current year as per matching principle of accounting.

Reflection in ledgers and financial statement:

Insurance Expense a/c

Date	Particular	$	Date	Particular	$
15/9/15	To bank	15,000	31/3/16	By insurance paid in advance	2,000
			31/3/16	**By P&L a/c**	**12,000**
		15,000			15,000

Insurance paid in advance a/c

Date	Particular	$	Date	Particular	$

31/3/16	To Insurance expense a/c	2,000	31/3/16	**By balance c/d**	**2,000**
		2,000			2,000

Profit and loss account

Expense	$	Income	$
Insurance a/c 15,000			
-Advance (2,000)	13,000		

Balance sheet

Asset	$	Liability	$
Insurance paid in advance	2,000		

4. Z ltd. has paid $60,000 as salary in financial year. It has $40,000 salary still payable at the end of the year.

Adjusting entry:

Journal entry	$	$
Salary a/c Dr	40,000	
To Salary payable a/c		40,000

Explanation: To adjust above transaction, we debit salary account by $40,000 and credit salary payable account. Debiting salary account increases expenses. We have yearend liability in form of salary which we record in accounting.

Reflection in Ledgers and financial statement:

Salary account

Date	Particular	$	Date	Particular	$
31/3/15	To bank a/c	60,000	31/3/15	**By P & L a/c**	**1,00,000**
31/3/15	To salary payable a/c	40,000			
		1,00,000			1,00,000

Salary Payable a/c

Date	Particular	$	Date	Particular	$
31/3/15	**To balance c/d**	**40,000**	31/3/15	By salary a/c	40,000
		40,000			40,000

Profit and loss account for the year....

Expenses	$	Income	$
Salary 60,000 +payable 40,000	1,00,000		

Balance sheet as on...

Asset	$	Liability	$
		Salary payable	40,000

5. Z Ltd. has $22,000 receivable. Among which, $2,000 is bad and it needs to be written off.

Adjustment entry:

Entry	$	$
Bad debt a/c Dr	2,000	
To debtor a/c		2,000

Explanation:

As bad debt is expense, debit entry is made and debtor account will be credited for that amount.

Reflection in ledgers and financial statement:

Bad debt

Date	Particular	$	Date	Particular	$
31/3/15	To debtor	2,000	31/3/15	BY P & L	2,000
		2,000			2,000

Debtor

Date	Particular	$	Date	Particular	$
10/4/14	To sales	22,000	31/3/15	By bad debt	2,000
			31/3/15	**By balance c/d**	**20,000**
		22,000			22,000

Profit and loss account for the year ending ...

Expense	$	Income	$
Bad debt	2,000		

Balance sheet as on...

Asset	$	Liability	$
Debtor 22,000 -Bad debt 2,000	20,000		

ADJUSTED TRIAL BALANCE

Adjusted trial balance is trial balance considering all the adjustment entries done in general ledger and prepared with new balances of general ledger.

Example:

Lets understand this concept with following example:

Unadjusted Trial balance as on 31/3/2016

Account	Dr	Cr
Building	1,00,000	
Stock	20,000	
Debtor	22,000	
Bank	2,12,000	
Creditor		35,000
Loan received		99,000
Sales		5,12,000
Purchase	3,22,000	
Salary	1,10,000	
Capital		1,40,000
	7,86,000	7,86,000

Following adjustments are pending on 31/3/2016:

1. Debtors worth $ 1200 are bad and company decides to write off them in current year.

2. It is policy of company to provide 10% depreciation on building at written down method.

3. Salary payable at year end is $10,000.

Exercise: Do adjusting entries for above transaction.

Ledgers with adjustment:

After considering all the adjustment, ledgers' balances will appear as follow:

Depreciation

Date	Particulars	$	Date	Particular	$
31/3/16	To building	10,000	31/3/16	By balance c/d	10,000
		10,000			10,000

Building

Date	Particulars	$	Date	Particular	$
1/4/15	To balance b/d	1,00,000	31/3/16	By depreciation	10,000
			31/3/16	By balance c/d	90,000
		1,00,000			1,00,000

Debtor

Date	Particular	$	Date	Particular	$
1/4/15	To sale	22,000	31/3/16	By bad debt	1,200
			31/3/16	By balance c/d	20,800
		22,000			22,000

Bad debt

Date	Particular	$	Date	Particular	$
31/3/16	To debtor	1,200			
		1,200			1,200

Salary a/c

Date	Particular	$	Date	Particular	$
30/3/16	To bank	1,10,000	31/3/16	By balance c/d	1,20,000
31/3/16	To salary payable	10,000			
		1,20,000			1,20,000

Salary payable a/c

Date	Particular	$	Date	Particular	$
31/3/16	By balance c/d	10,000	31/3/16	By salary a/c	10,000
		10,000			10,000

Transfer new adjusted balances to trial balance to prepare adjusted trial balance.

Adjusted trial balance as on 31/3/2016

Account	Dr	Cr
Building	**90,000**	
Stock	20,000	
Debtor	20,800	
Bank	2,12,000	
Creditor		35,000
Loan received		99,000
Sales		5,12,000
Purchase	3,22,000	
Salary	**1,20,000**	
Bad debt	**1,200**	
Depreciation	**10,000**	
Salary payable		**10,000**
Capital		1,40,000
	7,96,000	7,96,000

In big companies, there are lots of adjustments pending at year end. In that situation, accountant prepares 10 -column worksheet to cover all the adjustments.

PREPARATION OF 10 COLUMN WORKSHEET

10-column worksheet is statement that helps accountants plan and facilitate the end of period reporting process. It is not compulsory to prepare 10-column worksheet however it is advisable to prepare 10-column worksheet to reduce errors in doing end of period adjustments.

10-column worksheet structure:
As name suggests, there are 10 columns in 10-column worksheet covering following key areas:

1. Trial balance: All the accounts with corresponding balances are written in two columns.

2. Adjustment entries : These columns cover adjustments and involves such transactions as accruals, prepayment, depreciation adjustments.

3. Adjusted trial balance: These columns calculate new balances of ledger with adjustment.

4. Income statement: These columns record income and expenditure from adjusted trial balance. If total of income column exceeds total of expense column, the business has made profit. If total of expense column exceeds total of income column, company has made loss.

5. Balance sheet: These columns record assets, liabilities and equity balances from adjusted trial balance. Profit or loss made by business is recorded in equity account.

10-column worksheet

Following is the example of 10-column worksheet prepared year end.

Account	U.T.B		Adjustment		A.T.B		In. statement		B/S	
	Dr	Cr	Dr	Cr	Dr	Cr	Exp.	Income	Asset	Liability
Bank	2,22,000				2,22,000				2,22,000	
Car	4000			400	3600				3600	
Building	10,00,000			10,0000	90,0000				90,0000	
Investment	10,10,000				10,10,000				10,10,000	
Receivables	42,000			2,000	40,000				40,000	
Stock	52,000				52,000				52,000	
Loan from ABC bank		1,00,000	84,400			15,600				15,600
Payables		12,000				12,000				12,000
Bad debt	2,000				2,000		2,000			
Insurance paid in adv.	2,000				2,000				2,000	
Insurance exp	14,000			2,000	12,000		12,000			
Salary	1,20,000		20,000		1,40,000		1,40,000			

Salary payable		20,000				20,000				20,000
Sales		12,00,000				12,00,000		12,00,000		
Purchase	8,64,000				8,64,000		8,64,000			
Equity		20,00,000				20,00,000				20,00,000
Total	33,32000	33,32,000	20,000	1,04,400	32,47,600	32,47,600	10,18,000	12,00,000	22,29,600	20,47,600
Profit							1,82,000			1,82,000

Due to space, I have used small fonts. You can download worksheet in excel format from:

PREPARATION OF FINANCIAL STATEMENTS

Financial statements are financial information of business related to particular period presented in structured way.

Financial statements are helpful to internal and external parties related to business to gain insight about business profitability for relevant period and business position on specific date.

Financial statements cover following reports:

1. Profit and loss statement

2. Balance sheet

3. Change in owners' equity or capital account

4. Cash flow statement

Profit and loss statement:

Profit and loss account is the statement which summarizes the revenue, costs, expense during the specific period. Generally it is prepared quarterly or annually. This statement provides information about company's ability to generate profit. Profit and loss statement is also referred as income statement.

There are two formats of profit and loss account:

vertical Format

Profit and loss account for the year ended on ....

Particulars	($)
Sales	72,122
Other indirect income	12,000
	84122
Less cost of goods sold	32210
Selling and administrative expense	7212
Other operating expense	1200
Profit before interest	43500
Less interest	400
Profit after interest	43100
Less tax	12930
Profit after interest and taxes	**30,170**

Horizontal format:

Profit and loss account

Expense	$	Income	$
Opening stock	1,200	Sales	72,122
Purchase	33,200	Other income	12,000
Selling and administrative expense	7,212	Closing stock	2,190
Other expense	1,200		
Interest	400		
Tax	12,930		
Net profit	30,170		
	86,312		86,312

Balance sheet as on …:

Balance sheet is statement presenting business position on reporting date. It covers fixed assets, current assets, loan given, loan received, current liabilities, owner's equity.

Balance sheet has also two formats:

Horizontal format

Vertical format

Sample vertical format of balance sheet:

Balance sheet as on ....

Balance sheet			
	Note	As at 31 March	
		2015	2014
ASSETS			
Non-current assets			
Property		1,20,000	1,32,000
Intangible assets		10,000	12,000
Deferred income tax		2,000	1,000
Total non-current assets		1,32,000	1,45,000
Current assets			
Inventories		2,500	200
Trade and other receivables		13,000	11,200
Cash and cash equivalents		1,12,000	78,400
Total current assets		1,27,500	89,800
TOTAL ASSETS		2,59,500	2,34,800
EQUITY AND LIABILITIES			
Equity			
Share capital		1,00,000	80,000
Share premium			-
Other reserves		12,000	8,000
Retained earnings		1,12,000	84,220

Total equity		2,24,000	1,72,220
Liabilities			
Non-current liabilities			
Borrowings		37,500	40,000
Deferred income tax liabilities			
Provisions			
Total non-current liabilities		37,500	40,000
Current liabilities			
Payables		32,000	22,000
Current income tax liabilities			
Borrowings			
Provisions for other liabilites		2,000	1,620
Total current liabilities		34,000	23,620
Total liabilities		2,95,500	2,34,800
TOTAL EQUITY AND LIABILITIES		0	0

Sample Horizontal format of balance sheet:

Assets	$	Liabilities	$
Properties	1,20,000	Share capital	1,00,000
Intangible assets	10,000	Share premium	12,000
Deferred income tax	2,000	Retained earnings	1,12,000
Inventories	2,500	Borrowings	37,500
Trade and other receivables	13,000	Payable	32,000
Cash and cash equivalents	1,12,000	Provisions for other liabilities	2,000

Total	2,95,500	Total	2,95,500

Owners' equity or capital account:

In sole proprietorship, Owner's equity presents owner's contribution in business less withdrawal during the year add/less profit earned / loss incurred during the year.

Ferry's shop

Owners' equity

Capital of Ferry	$1,00,000	
Add Additional capital introduced during the year	$25,000	
Add Total profit earned during the year	$59,000	$1,84,000
Less Drawing	$8,000	$8,000
Closing capital at the end of the year		$1,76,000

For corporate, owner's equity means sum of share capital issued, retained earnings and other accumulated reserves.

XYZ PVT Ltd.

Statement of Owners' equity

Particulars	$
Paid in share capital	10,00,000
Paid in share capital in excess of par	2,50,000

value	
Retained earning	3,00,000
Accumulated other income	12,000
Total equity fund	**15,62,000**

As per GAAP principle, it is required to prepare statement of change in owners' equity to present details about movement in reserves during the year. It covers following:

1. Net profit / loss during the year
2. Increase / decrease of share capital
3. Capital gains
4. Effect in change of accounting policies or procedures
5. Dividend payments

XYZ Ltd.

Statement of change in equity for the year ended 31/3/2015

	Share capital	Retained earning	Revaluation surplus	Total equity
Balance as on 1st Apr, 2014	12,00,000	1,25,000	0	13,25,000
Changes in equity for the year 2014-15				
Change in accounting policy	–	–	–	–
Issue of share capital	2,00,000		–	2,00,000
Revaluation of asset			22,000	22,000
Profit earned during year		2,12,000		2,12,000
Dividend		(12,000)		(12,000)
Balance as on 31/3/15	14,00,000	3,25,000	22,000	**17,47,000**

Foot note under balance sheet:

There is also section of foot note under balance sheet to show following:

1. Major accounting policies followed by company during the year

2. Contingent liabilities as on balance sheet date.

3. Any information which can effect investors' decision and going concern of business.

CASH FLOW STATEMENT:

Cash flow statement is prepared to present cash movement in business for specific period. It reports activities of cash generation and cash utilization in business. Cash flow statement is one of the main financial statements.

It covers three activities:
1. Operating activities: It presents the items of operating activities in cash. All non cash items are added back or deducted from operating profit.
2. Investing activities: It reports activities of purchase and sale of fixed assets and investments during the reporting period.
3. Financial activities: It reports issue of shares, bonds, debentures and repurchase or redemption of the same. It also covers activities of borrowing of loan and repayment of loan.
4. Additional information: It reports the amount of taxes and interest paid. Other important non- cash items are also reported in this section.

Benefits of preparation of cash flow statement:
1. It is useful to know about liquidity of assets of company and capacity of company to pay dividend, buy back of shares or acquire another company.
2. It is useful to determine ability of company to generate profit from operating activities.

How to prepare cash flow statement:

Remember following simple rules to prepare cash flow statement easily.
1. When asset increases, cash account decreases.
2. When asset decreases, cash account increases.

3. When liability increases, cash account increases.
4. When liability decreases, cash account decreases.
5. When capital increases, cash account increases.
6. When owner's equity increases, cash account decreases.

IMP note: cash means cash, bank and cash equivalent.
1. Any change in current assets or current liabilities should be reported in operating activities.
2. Any change in fixed assets (Long term assets) or investment should be reported in investing activities.
3. Any change in long term liabilities and shareholder's equity should be reported in financial activities.

There are two methods to prepare cash flow statement:
1. Direct Method
2. Indirect Method

Direct Method:

In this method, cash flow from operative activities displays the net amount of cash that was received or disbursed during the given period of time.

Following format can be used to prepare cash flow from direct method:

Cash flow from operating activities	$	
Cash sales	1,00,000	
Cash collected from customer	1,12,220	
Cash paid to supplier	(70,121)	
Cash purchase	(8,000)	

Cash paid to employees	(20,000)	
Cash payments for operating expenses	(12,000)	
Interest payment	(3,500)	98,599
Cash flow from investing activities		
Cash received from sale of asset	1,15,000	
Cash paid to purchase asset	(30,200)	84,800
Cash flow from financial activities		
Proceeds for loan	50,000	
Repayment from loan	(2,000)	
Proceeds from issue of shares	10,000	
Payment to repurchase shares	0	
Payment to repurchase debenture	(5,000)	
Proceed from issue of debentures	15,000	68,000
Net increase in cash		2,51,399
Opening cash and cash equivalent		45,200
Closing cash and cash equivalent		2,96,599

Generally accounts are not maintained on cash basis so it is time consuming to find out cash from operating activities using direct method. Remember following rules when you are preparing cash flow from operating activities using direct method.

Cash received from customers =

Opening balance + Credit sales - Bad debt- closing balance

Customer's a/c / receivables

Opening balance		Money received from customer	?
Credit sales		Bad debt	
		Closing balance	

Cash paid to suppliers:

To find out payment made supplier, we need to find credit purchase from inventory account.

Credit purchase = cost of goods sold + closing stock – opening stock – cash purchase

From credit purchase, we can find payment made to supplier.

Payment to supplier = Closing balance of supplier – opening balance – credit purchase.

Supplier account

Payments	?	Opening balance	
Closing balance		Credit purchase	?

Inventory account

Opening balance		Cost of goods sold	
Cash purchase			
Credit purchase		Closing stock	

In this way, by preparing ledger account or using formulas we can find missing figures to use direct method.

Indirect method to prepare cash flow statement:

Generally indirect method is used to prepare cash flow statement because accrual accounting is followed in most of businesses.

To prepare cash flow from operating activities as per indirect method, we begin with net profit taken from income statement and do adjustments to arrive cash flow from operating activity.

Steps to prepare cash flow from operating activities:
1. Star with net profit as per P&L account
2. Add non cash expenses
3. Add / Less loss on sale of asset and profit on sale of asset
4. Account for changes in all current assets and current liabilities.

Format of cash flow statement prepared under indirect method:

Net profit	1,20,000
Add depreciation	2,000
Add non cash expenses	1,000
Add loss on sale of asset	500
Less profit on sale of asset	0
Add decrease in current asset	1000
Less increase in current asset	(2000)
Add increase in current liability	9000
Less decrease in current liability	(2000)
Cash flow from operating activities	129500
Sale of asset	40,000
Less purchase of asset	(60,000)
Cash flow from investing activities	(20,000)
Proceeds from issue of shares	50,000
Less Payment to repurchase share	0
Proceeds from issue of debenture	10,000
Less Payment to repurchase debenture	
Loan taken	0
Less loan repaid	(20,000)

Cash flow from financial activities	40,000
Net cash flow	1,49,500
Add cash and cash equivalent at the beginning of the year	25,000
Closing cash and cash equivalent at the closing of the year	1,74,500

Difference between direct and indirect method to prepare cash flow statement is preparation of cash flow from operating activities. In computerized environment, preparation of financial statements are done automatically in software but having basic knowledge to prepare the statements clear your accounting concept and increase your accuracy in work.

Closing of accounts:
Last step in accounting cycle is to do closing journal entries. All the temporary accounts' balances are transferred to permanent accounts.

Temporary accounts:
Temporary accounts are income accounts to track accounting activity during the year. Example: revenue and expense accounts.

Permanent accounts:
Permanent accounts are balance sheet accounts that are

used to track accounting activities that last longer than a year. Example: Fixed asset account that is recorded on balance in balance sheet.

Here is the sequence of the closing process:
1. Close the revenue accounts to profit and loss account or income account.
2. Close the expense accounts to profit and loss account or income account.
3. Close the income account to the retained earnings or capital account.

At the end of the year, revenue and expenses are closed to income account to make their balance zero at the start of the year. In this way, matching principle is followed.

Closing entries:

Account name	Debit	Credit
Agency income a/c Dr	1,00,000	
To Profit and loss a/c		1,00,000

All the incomes are transferred to profit and loss account this way.

Account name	Debit	Credit
Profit and loss a/c Dr	25,200	
To wages a/c		200
To salary a/c		5,000
To rent a/c		12,000

To interest a/c		2,000
To depreciation a/c		6,000
Account name	Debit	Credit
Retained earning / Capital account	1200	
To Withdrawal a/c / Dividend a/c		1200

Since dividend or withdrawal is not expense of business but withdrawal by owner of business, this account is transferred to retained earnings or capital account.

Account	Debit	Credit
P&L a/c Dr / Income summary a/c Dr	74,800	
To Retained earning a/c / capital a/c		74,800

After doing all the closing entries, Income summary account has balance equal to net profit for the year. This balance is transferred to retained earnings or capital account.

POST CLOSING TRIAL BALANCE

The post closing trial balance is a list of accounts after doing all the closing entries. In this account, all permanent accounts and their balances are presented. It is identical to accounts presented in balance sheet.

Purpose of preparation of post closing trial balance:

Main purpose of preparation of post closing trial balance is to verify that all the temporary accounts are closed properly and debits and credits are equal after closing books.

Format of post closing trial balance:

Post closing trial balance has same format as trial balance. There are three columns: account name, debit and credit.

Order of accounts is assets, liabilities and equity.

Example of post closing trial balance:

Account	Debit	Credit
Cash	20,000	
Bank	1,31,200	
Inventory	12,000	
Plant	1,12,000	
Tools	33,220	
Prepaid insurance	1,000	
Receivable	33,150	
Payables		42,205
Accumulated depreciation		11,200
Loan received		1,15,000
Retained earning		1,31,595
Bills payable		42,570
Total	3,42,570	3,42,570

FINAL WORDS FROM AUTHOR!

Hi,

Congratulations on finishing this book. I hope this book has helped you in testing of your accounting knowledge.

Please Don't forget to rate this book on Amazon.

You can buy my other books on amazon and accounting course on udemy.

Please follow the links:

Book – Accounting workbook – 200+ Questions and Answers - https://www.amazon.com/dp/B01LXLYDYI

Udemy course - https://www.udemy.com/accounting-for-beginners-how-to-do-accounting-super-easily/?couponCode=AMAZONGIFT

(50% Off – Purchase at $10)

Best wishes for your future.

Tarannum

Made in United States
Troutdale, OR
11/21/2023

14805087R00046